Lessons From the Heart:

How I Found Meaning For My Life From My Dying Mother

Angie Steele

Lessons From the Heart: How I Found Meaning For My Life From My Dying Mother

Copyright © 2014 by Angie Steele

All rights reserved, including but not limited to the right to reproduce this work in whole or in part in any form whatsoever; the right to store this material in or introduce it into a retrieval system; and the right to transmit this material in any form by any electronic, mechanical, photocopying, recording or other means without the express prior written permission of the copyright owner and the publisher of this book.

ISBN 978-0-9899063-1-9 (pbk)
ISBN 978-9899063-0-2 (eBook)

Printed in the United States

Cover design by: Lipstick & Rouge Designs

Dedication

To my beautiful son, Caleb, your unconditional love inspires me to keep moving forward.

Table of Contents

Introduction   6

Lesson 1: Love Is a Verb: People Know They're Loved When You Show Them in Words and Deeds   9

Lesson 2: Kids Are Inspired More by What You Do As a Parent Than by What You Say   17

Lesson 3: Grieve Over the Death of a Loved One, Embrace Their Memory, and Move on with Your Life   22

Lesson 4: In All Things Proceed with Excellence, Grace, and Wisdom   28

Lesson 5: Never Give Up on Your Dreams   31

Lesson 6: Speak Positive Affirmations over Yourself on a Daily Basis   33

Lesson 7: Not Going to Church Isn't an Option If You're Going to Live in My House   36

Lesson 8: Behold the Beauty in All Things   39

Lesson 9: The Power of Giving   42

Lesson 10: Gratitude Is an Attitude, and Practice   45
Makes Perfect

About the Author   49

Introduction

This book is designed to help you who are struggling with the death of a loved one and are now trying to find meaning in your life as a result of the emptiness you feel from being left behind.

My Mom, Marjorie Mercer, died on September 28, 2007, from colon cancer. She was sixty-five years old. The last four months of her life were painfully debilitating yet spiritually enlightening for me.

A few weeks before she died, she asked me to stay with her. She said, "It'll only be for a little while, so you don't have to quit your job. Just take a leave of absence." And she even offered to pay my bills while I was with her. I had just started a contract job as a technical recruiter, so I didn't have the luxury of being able to take leave. My only option was to quit. So I quit to move back home to be with my mother. My attitude was, "I only have one mom"; so when she asked me to do something as important as what she was asking, I made the only decision I felt I could make.

What I soon discovered when my Mom asked me to stay with her was that she wasn't asking me to take care of her physically because she had many more capable caregivers than I could ever be. That set-up was all spiritual. Indeed, what she did was to pass on to me a spiritual mantle. The mantle represented the responsibility that I now had to live the life that she had helped to prepare me for. What a profound revelation for me.

For months after my Mom died, I felt a huge void, and I struggled to find real meaning for my life. But after much prayer and reflection, what helped me get through that difficult time was writing down the thoughts I had about my Mom and how she helped to add value to my life. As a result, I ended up with this book, which includes a few of the lessons she taught me throughout my life. I discovered that if I focused on moving forward, capitalizing on the lessons that she taught me, there was a good chance that I would be okay—not only okay, but that I would actually thrive. The ten lessons in this first edition are not in the order in which they occurred in my life but are rather representative of a process I call random reflection.

Little did I know at the time of my growing up that it was my Mom's great master plan to prepare me for the rest of my life without her by imparting these life lessons. I am so blessed to have had a mother like Marjorie Mercer. I recall my Mom saying on many occasions that I had to learn how to do certain things for myself because she wouldn't always be around to help me. I didn't understand the real meaning of what she was trying to convey because—let's face it—as a child you think your parents are going to live forever; at least you don't think about the fact that one day they might not be. Nevertheless, I took heed of the lessons and the teachings that my mother was trying her very best to convey. I made a lot of mistakes along the road; but all in all, I turned out to be a very responsible and happy adult. I now have a child of my own, and I'm teaching him some of those same lessons that my Mom taught me.

    Enjoy the book, and I hope that you learn how to find meaning for your life after the death of a loved one.

Lesson 1: Love Is a Verb: People Know They're Loved When You Show Them in Words and Deeds

My beloved Mom was one of ten children who grew up on a farm in eastern North Carolina. It was in that close-knit rural community that she learned very early the importance of sharing, hard work, and family. She was raised by two loving and hardworking parents, Charlie and Louise Hughes. Charlie and Louise were the epitome of love, generosity, and compassion. They loved people, and it showed in how they lived their lives. They would often take in elderly people from the community to come and live with them when they got too old or too sick to care for themselves. So my Mom learned from her parents about how to care for other people. This was a trait that she would pass on to me as well. She had a life-long passion for helping people, young and old alike.

Two of the elderly people whom my grandparents took in and whom I remember fondly are Uncle Pete and Miss Essie. Uncle Pete was my Grandmother Louise's uncle, her mother's brother. Uncle Pete lived with his wife Annie about a half a mile up the road when he was in good health; but when my Grandmother Louise noticed that dementia was setting in, she offered him to come live with her and her family so she could help take care of him. She knew that within a short span of time, his condition would worsen and the time would come when he would remember less and less and would therefore need hands-on care.

    I was about seven years old at the time, but I have fond and vivid memories of Uncle Pete. He was a light-skinned man, small in stature, soft spoken, very easy going, and quite pleasant. His sharp facial features made him very easy to look at, and so I can imagine that he may have been quite popular with the ladies back in his heyday. By the time he came to live with my grandparents, he was already in his eighties, so he moved around very slowly. In fact, I remember that it would take him forever to do anything because when he walked, he would take small baby steps. I can see him now sitting in a chair and wearing khaki pants and his old-man sweater. Uncle Pete would live with my grandparents until he died.

    When my grandparents found out that you were in trouble, if offering you a place to stay and a free meal would help, they had no problem extending the invitation, which is what they did with Miss Essie. After church on Sundays, they would drive around visiting different folks in the neighborhood, especially those they hadn't seen in a few weeks. When they were to stop in on Miss Essie, what they would come to find was disturbing and sad. On this particular visit, they discovered a disoriented old lady, abandoned by a relative, living in a house in great disrepair, no food, no electricity, and tattered clothing. My Granddaddy Charlie simply asked, "Miss Essie, do you want to come home with us?" and she responded yes. She stayed with my family for about eight years until she died. She, too, suffered from dementia. Miss Essie was a strange bird, unlike Uncle Pete; she was not mild mannered and easy going, especially in her latter years. She was loud, demanding, and mentally unstable. Her frequent outbursts would startle guests and frustrate my aunts, who would help their mother care for Miss Essie.

    Because my grandparents put into action their love, it gave my mother a concrete example of love to follow. Just like my grandmother, my Mom lived to help people. It's a trait that I witnessed in my Mom for as long as I can remember; and although she didn't bring people into our home to care for them, she always found a way to help people in need. She would tell me all the time that I should do nice things for people whenever I could, and to do them without cost to the individual. I wasn't allowed to accept money when I gave rides to people, ran errands for them, or did household chores.

Because of the example my grandparents set for my Mother in caring for people, it was only natural for my Mom to take on the role of caretaker for her mother when she had heart surgery and then a stroke.

It wasn't until my Mom retired from Elizabeth City State University that she embarked upon her third career as a caregiver. She would now go into the homes of the people she cared for. She would cook, clean, take her patients to their doctor's appointments, but most of all she would spend time talking with them. Her patients were elderly, and some of them would die in my Mother's care; and that would make it all the more difficult because they became like members of our family.

It's ironic how much we pattern our lives after our parents, sometimes without even realizing it. When my Mom became sick from colon cancer, I spent the last few months of her life providing care for her. When I think about what it was like spending time with my Mom, knowing that in just a few short months, the person whom I loved and adored and freely trusted to mold and shape my life would be gone, never to return again on this earth, I remember how it was overwhelmingly sad and frustrating, to say the least.

I experienced the greatest joy and the greatest tragedy all in the same few months, while caring for my Mom. I knew that the end was drawing near for her. Her physical body had dwindled down to almost nothing but a mere skeleton. She used to shriek with pain when the home health nurse would turn her to bathe her, but during the final week that loud shriek was just a faint moan. Her mouth would open, but hardly any sound would come out. Again, this was confirmation for me that her final days were fast approaching, and so I felt my role changing from caretaker to just becoming a witness of the transition from life to death that was occurring in front of me. I knew that there was nothing more that I could do for my mother's physical body. I was now dissolving her pain medication, which had switched from Percocet to Oxycodone, in water and feeding it to her from a spoon, as that was the only way that she could accept it. She would sleep most of the day, and when she was awake, there was just a blank stare. But sometimes her eyes would follow me across the room, and I would wonder what she was thinking and what unspoken words she had left to share with me. I felt helpless in not being able to do anything more to help my Mom. It was amazing to me to observe how quickly the human body can decline when it's riddled with a terminal disease. There was also a sense of relief knowing that she would soon be out of her pain and misery.

I would sit quietly and ponder why God would allow my Mom to die in such a seemingly ungraceful way, and the answer I got was, "Why not your Mother?" When I look at the life of my Mom, I think of someone who almost always followed the rules. My Mom rarely ruffled any feathers, spoke out of turn, or had many negative words to say about anyone. She was a good person who was adored by many. For those reasons and many more, I felt like she had more people to help and more good deeds to accomplish. The epiphany I had is that it's never about the individual's bucket list, but it's about what God wants to do through the life of that individual; and when God determines that He has accomplished what He set out to do with your life, He has all the power to call you home, thus ending your life here on earth. The sooner I got that revelation, the sooner I was able to let my Mom go and look forward to what God had purposed for my life and the life of others. Before I discovered the true purpose for my life, I used to think that my life was my own and that I could do with it just what I wanted to. But what I came to realize is that all of my actions have consequences, good and bad, and that I'm accountable to other people for my behavior. Now I make choices that are aligned with my purpose and vision. I think my Mom lived her life in that same way.

My Mom was one who never complained and always embraced the good with the bad and somehow always managed to make sense of it all; what she couldn't make sense of, she left it for God to sort out. And I felt this experience was no different for her. My Mom was a good patient. She showed me she loved me one last time when she chose to give me the gift of spiritual enlightenment instead of focusing on her own mortality in her final days. My Mom had accepted that she was going to die, so rather than focus on a situation that she could not change, she focused on executing the final phase of her plan for my life. The first thing my Mom did was to make sure that we could be together, so she made me an offer that I couldn't refuse by asking me to move in with her temporarily and take care of her while offering to pay bills, if I did so. I couldn't turn down that offer. While my Mom's physical body was getting weaker and weaker, I sensed that her spirit was getting stronger and was calling out to me and to anyone who was receptive. While my Mom wasn't talking a lot during the last few weeks, she did talk some, but most of what I picked up from her was nonverbal through her eyes and her body language. I could read her eyes like the pages in a book, and

I would find myself asking my Mom a series of questions trying to make sure that I was fulfilling her request as she was suggesting. And I remember one time sensing her say to me, "Now what are you going to do?" That question caused me to ponder the obvious, "What do you mean, what am I going to do?" I remember taking a few minutes to try to answer that question in my head with several different scenarios; and after coming up with nothing that made sense based on recent interactions between me and my Mom, a light bulb went off in my head, and I thought she must mean What Am I Going to Do with the Rest of My Life. And when I looked up at my Mom with my newfound revelation, I saw in her eyes a look of approval, as if to say, "Now You're on to Something." That was an a-ha moment for me, and one that I didn't take lightly because it would change the course of my existence and the reason for being in my Mom's presence at this appointed time. From then on I paid close attention to my thoughts and closer attention to my interaction with my Mom, and I began journaling to capture my thoughts and sensings from my Mom. That time with my Mom was a spiritual awakening for me, to say the least.

Lesson 2: Kids Are Inspired More by What You Do As a Parent Than by What You Say

Be a "Positive Example Parent"

My Mom taught me early on that kids learn more by watching their parents than they do by listening to their parents. She was a shining example of someone who walked out every lesson she passed on to me. I used to listen closely to her conversations to see if she would tell her friends one thing and do another, but she never did. My mom would often make offers to do nice things for people, like cook, clean, run errands, give rides, visit, etc., and she would actually do what she promised she would do; and if for some reason she couldn't follow through, she would call to negotiate another time that was mutually suitable.

My Mom passed down many lessons on being a "positive example parent," like the time when she decided she wanted a separation from my Dad. The news didn't go over well with my Dad or my Dad's mother (Cora). My Grandmother Cora, as a result, had some not-so-nice things to say about my Mother; and instead of directing her frustration and concerns to my Mother, she felt it appropriate to express her feelings to me. Well, as a child, I was really upset to have someone whom I loved say unkind things about someone else whom I loved, namely, my Mother. I went home in tears trying my best to explain what just happened to my Mother. She understood enough of what I was saying to know that her mother-in-law was bad-mouthing her. I told my Mother that she must go over right now and explain her side of the story to my grandmother so that the truth would be known. My Mom in a calm voice told me that she was not going over to explain anything to anybody because it wasn't anyone's concern, and she went on to say that in time the truth about her marriage would be revealed. At the time, I totally disagreed with her logic, but since that was her marriage and not mine, she was the mother and I was the child, and I knew my place, I kept the rest of my comments to myself. However, afterward, I found it very difficult to even visit my grandmother because of the not so nice things she said about my mother. It was my Mother who insisted that I let go of the anger and hostility I felt toward my grandmother at that time and that I go over and visit. My Mother would say, "But, that's your grandmother, and you'll be a better person if you forgive her and move past this situation." At first, I refused; then at my Mother's constant urging, I gave in and would go over for a visit with my grandma. I didn't know at the time what the lesson was in that tense family moment. I was just being obedient to the command of my Mother. Now, I fully understand the lesson my Mom was conveying. My Mom, in all of her grace and wisdom, didn't react negatively when she was talked about and falsely accused, but instead she held her head up high and stayed focused on the things that were positive, and that would be how I watched her live her life even toward the end.

I know now that being a mom is the most important job I'll ever be blessed to have. I have an eleven-year-old son whom I love and adore; therefore, it is important to me that my son looks up to me as one who keeps her word. My son Caleb is the light of my life, and my goal is to pass on to him the values that my mom passed on to me. Since I am one of his primary role models, I am constantly concerned about making good decisions because I know he's watching me and taking notes on how I do things, not just what I say. Being a "positive example parent" doesn't mean that you don't make mistakes; instead, it means you live life with integrity even when no one is watching.

In the last few months of my Mother's life, I witnessed her struggle with doing the basics like walking, sitting up, eating, bathing, and dressing herself. She required the help of others to accomplish the smallest tasks. Yet even in her struggle to manage the basics, she never complained. My Mom thought that complaining was a misplaced use of time. She thought, in general, that while you were spending time complaining, you could have either completed the task or made some headway getting something else meaningful done. So rather than complain about her health situation, she decided to focus her energy on being healed; and then later when it was clear to her that her health would not get better, I believe she focused on completing one of her final assignments here on earth. And that was making sure that her life and death struggles would not be in vain. For you see, she understood that when you focus on the prize of the high calling and not the petty things of life, or the things that you cannot change, you stand a great chance of touching the lives of others in very meaningful ways; and that was what she wanted of our last few months together. If I didn't get it before, I get it now—what my Mom meant by focusing on the prize of the high calling. I believe the high calling for my Mom was training me up in the way that I should go. I believe she knew that once she deposited the seeds of wisdom and knowledge into my life, I would feel obligated to do something with them and not let them die, which is why I believe that my Mom is never far away from me—for the very reason to watch over the seeds. When I think about the significance of my Mom's journey through life and the pain and suffering she endured, I feel a great eagerness to accomplish what I believe I was put here on earth to do.

It takes courage and conviction to be a Positive Example Parent. It means that you live your life with a high level of discipline while adhering to a set of principles that you've determined are the best for guiding yourself and your family on a path to a successful life. My Mom made some mistakes along the way, but she didn't focus on her mistakes; instead, she mustered up the courage to be the one to set an example for me and others to follow even in the very end, thus giving me the chance to reach my fullest potential. This is the example she lived for me, even in her journey to death.

Lesson 3: Grieve Over the Death of a Loved One, Embrace Their Memory, and Move on with Your Life

The Death of My Parents

The death of a parent is one of the toughest challenges you'll ever face, I know firsthand. My parents died ten years apart. My Dad died first on May 3, 1997, from lung cancer. He had always been a smoker for as long as I can remember. His cigarette brand of choice was Viceroy. He started when he was about fourteen years old and smoked all the way through his Army days and all of his adult life until he died at the age of sixty-five. Ironically, he died at the same age as his father and from the same dreadful disease. Unlike my Mom, my Dad lived for only two weeks after he was diagnosed, so he didn't suffer like my Mom. That was a blessing.

My Dad grew up in eastern North Carolina in a small family with one sister. He had lots of cousins around to play with, though; and he was very close to his father. When my Dad was younger, he enjoyed playing baseball and was pretty good at it, I'm told. Among his other interests were playing the piano, the guitar, and a love for nice cars. He was a man of few words, so getting him to share anything, let alone glimpses of himself, was a challenge. What I do know is that he spent a couple years in the Army from 1954 to 1956, and after returning home, he would spend time tending the family farm. But when he married my Mom, he needed to earn more money, so he began working for a larger farm owner in the town. A few years after my brother and I were born, my Mom encouraged him to get a job as a long shoreman. My Mom had brothers and uncles who worked with the HRSA-ILA (International Long Shoreman Association), so she knew the pay was better as well as the other benefits (union, pension, health insurance, etc.).

    I made the comment when my Dad died, "Losing a father is hard enough, but I don't know if I could withstand the pain if my Mom dies before I do." Little did I know that I would have ten more years to spend with my Mom before she would die, too. My Mom was seemingly very healthy. I never really saw her overeat; when she was full, she got up from the table. She was the epitome of the saying, "Life, be in it." She led a very active and, again, healthy lifestyle by walking and being mindful of what and how much she ate. My mother got regular checkups at the doctor, except she mentioned one time that no one had ever encouraged her to have a colonoscopy done, and she never did.

In 2004, she had the worse stomach ache that she said she had ever had. It kept her up all night. The next morning, she went to the doctor and got checked out, and they found blockage in her intestines. The doctors labeled it colon cancer. She went through her surgery with flying colors and recovered very nicely. Within just a few days of being home from the hospital, she was moving about and cooking. My Mom was not a woman you could hold down; she had to stay busy doing things and helping out in some way. I took the week off from my business to spend with her as she recuperated from surgery; and toward the end of the week, I was doing very little for my Mom. She insisted that she do things for herself because that was the only way she was going to get stronger. That week was one of the best weeks of my life. I enjoyed being back home and visiting with my family. I got to spend some quality time with my Mom, which was priceless, and I also spent some time with my Granddaddy Charlie as he would stop by every morning to check on my Mom. I ran errands for Mom and ran into old friends while I was out and about; it was fabulous. I think that life is easy back in eastern North Carolina. I brought my laptop, and fortunately I was able to manage my work schedule while caring for my Mother.

Although my Mom recovered nicely from the surgery, when she had her follow up CT scan, it showed that the cancer had spread to her liver, which is never a good sign. The doctor wanted her to start chemotherapy right away, and she did. However, after a couple of years on and off the treatment, there was no change in the CT scan, so the doctor indicated that there was nothing more that could be done. But I didn't take that negative response for an answer. In 2007, I set out to put my Mom on a holistic medical plan complete with a diet of fruits and vegetables. I purchased over $500 in holistic medicine that my Mom would take. I even found a doctor in Marietta, Georgia, who treated all sorts of illnesses and diseases using a holistic approach. Dr. David Lee of the Wellness Revolution Clinic is a trained chiropractor and uses all kinds of laser technology to heal the entire body. I rented an RV, hired a retired nurse and a nurse's aid to travel with me, and got on the road to Marietta to see the doctor who was going to help my mother get well. My brother Anthony also went with us to drive. It was such a blessing to have him come along on the trip. My Mom was a trooper—she took that nine-hour ride like a champ.

Dr. Lee's office was the first doctor's office that I had ever seen that formed a circle with the patients and prayed every morning before he performed a single procedure that day. It was like nothing I had ever experienced. She would receive two treatments per day, usually one in the morning and then one in the afternoon. The treatments would help her some, but in reality the disease that would ultimately take my Mom had progressed to the point where her organs were too fragile. Nevertheless, she left Georgia much stronger than when she went.

    I believe that my Mom was in a state of contentment despite the sickly condition she was in. Eventually, she would suffer from severe back pain because the cancer cells were pushing out her disks and causing great pain and discomfort. We were allowed to keep a laser machine from a local doctor over the weekend to treat the pain, and that seemed to help some; but eventually what would happen is that the only thing that would keep my Mom comfortable would be the high doses of Oxycodone that she would have to take around the clock in order to keep the pain from taking over. By that time, Hospice had already been called in to be a part of my Mom's life for the final weeks to help with the transition. Before my Mom began experiencing the constant pain, I still believed that she would get better. But much to my disappointment, she never did, and she died on September 28, 2007. I was very fortunate, though, because unlike with my Dad, I got to spend the last few months of my Mom's life with her. I remember asking Mom after her mother died if she missed her mom, and she replied, "I certainly do, and not a day goes by that I don't think about her. But I can't stay sad forever. I have to move on with my life. Mama would want it that way." I have adopted that same philosophy in dealing with the loss of my parents. What has helped me to move on with my life is, first, making a conscious decision to grieve and move forward; second, journaling my feelings (the good ones, the bad ones, and the indifferent ones) and mapping out a strategic plan for my life; and third, holding steadfast to my faith and trusting that God would comfort and strengthen me when I needed it the most.

Lesson 4: In All Things Proceed with Excellence, Grace, and Wisdom

Learning to Do Things Right

My Mom worked during an era when you were rewarded for company loyalty. She worked twenty-five years with cabinet maker IXL and another twenty years as a state employee at Elizabeth City State University. What I learned from my Mother professionally was that no matter what your line of work, you have to perform your duties in excellence. So often my Mother would make me go back and redo tasks big and small because I did them sloppily or half-heartedly. I remember once I decided to take on the ambitious project of sewing my own outfit. My Mom was a good seamstress, but I didn't have the patience for sewing. Every five minutes I would scream to my Mom in the next room, "Now what do I do?" Two or three times she would answer my question; but the fourth time, she yelled back, "You're smart, figure it out yourself!" Well, I took the lazy route and ended up sewing the collar to the arm hole instead of the neck hole. Even though I took it as just another home-economic project, my Mom took exception to that notion and made me undo my sloppy work and do it the correct way. She said that I had to learn how to complete tasks in excellence as that would be the foundation on which I would build a successful career and life.

When I think about the last few weeks of my Mom's life, while I didn't see her complete tasks, I saw evidence of completed tasks done with grace, wisdom, and in excellence. For example, my Mom's business affairs were in impeccable order. Because of her long-term employment with the state of North Carolina, she maintained good health insurance and a nice pension. She also had in place more than enough life insurance, other private investments, real estate, and an ample cash savings in the bank. All of her important documents were kept in a black briefcase that she stored in the back of her closet. As a result of my Mom's savvy financial planning and disciplined lifestyle, she provided the means to take care of herself during her illness, so that it did not cause a financial hardship for me or my brother or anyone else placed in the position to have to care for her. It allowed her to remain in her own home and transition peacefully.

I now teach my son the same valuable lesson on completing tasks in excellence. For example, I will make him erase a whole paragraph and rewrite it if it has misspelled words or the sentence structure is not clear. He hates when I make him do work over, but afterward he appreciates having put in the extra effort when his teacher gives him an A for his writing. I can relate to the frustration because I would get upset at my Mom when she would insist that my work was subpar and have me do it over and over again until I got it right. However, I appreciate her persistence in teaching me to always do my best and let my results speak for themselves. I have carried those foundational principles of doing my best work with me throughout my career and my life, and I am amazed at the overwhelming sense of accomplishment I get when I know I did my best. My Mom sacrificed a lot (as all good mothers do) for me and my brother, so I feel like I honor her life when I constantly seek to fulfill her philosophy of learning to do things right.

Lesson 5: Never Give Up on Your Dreams

The Best Career Move of My Life

Ever since I was a child, my Mom would tell me that I could do anything I wanted to do in life. She would say you're smart, you're pretty, and all you need to do is work hard, and you will accomplish great things. She would tell me to be sure to develop good and consistent work habits, and opportunities would beat a path to my door.

All things happen for a reason, and being laid off in 2004 was, in hindsight, no accident; it turned out to be one of the best things that's ever happened to me career-wise. It was then that I took it as a sign from God that I was now supposed to start my own business and become an entrepreneur. It was then that the journey would lead to my freedom. My friend Jonathan had been telling me for years that I was supposed to be an entrepreneur and start my own business, but I kept replying, "No, you don't understand. I'm quite content working this job that I love." I would say, "One entrepreneur in the family is quite enough," because at the time I was married to Stephen, who had always been in business for himself. Finally, in 2004, I responded to a nudge and took the challenge to start my own business. Now, who knows how long it would have taken me if I hadn't been laid off because at the time I was earning a six-figure income. After putting out my shingle, I started working as a media consultant with a very successful speaker, bestselling author, certified personal and executive coach. As entrepreneurs sometimes do, I stopped and started a lot, course corrected some, and there were times when I went back to my old profession in Human Resources as a technical recruiter, which I happen to enjoy a lot. Other titles I've held are virtual assistant, real estate investor, writer, and producer of children's entertainment. During the process of becoming a successful entrepreneur, I've had some ups and some downs, but all in all I am an entrepreneur.

My Mom taught me to try different things and to never give up on my dreams. My dreams now are to become a celebrated author, produce animated entertainment for children, and teach business skills to other entrepreneurs. My Mom assured me before she died that I would reach each one of my goals if I keep moving forward, believe in myself, and have confidence in the people who will be sent along to help me. "Just have faith, work hard, and be consistent," she said. And that's how I pursue my dreams. I am now looking for office space to house my media and education conglomerate.

Lesson 6: Speak Positive Affirmations over Yourself on a Daily Basis

The Relationship You Have with Yourself Is Important Too

It was from my Mom that I learned the concept of treating myself well; and that, she said, will set the standard for how well others treat you. Treating yourself well begins with nurturing yourself emotionally and physically. My mom always fed herself with positive self-talk. She had a very positive mental attitude, and she rarely said a negative word about anyone. In fact, one of her nieces commented once that if you want to know the town gossip, don't call Aunt Margie because you won't get it. That was a compliment to my Mom's character. She was an example of how to be nice and respectful of other people. My Mom felt that if you showed a good measure of kindness and forgiveness to yourself that it would be much easier to extend that same grace to others. It would allow you to forgive and accept others' mistakes and unfortunate circumstances more easily and to be less judgmental because after all you could find yourself or someone close to you in a very similar situation.

My Mom fed me with positive affirmations as well—she would always tell me that I could do anything I set my mind to do and that I was beautiful. I believe that wholeheartedly now, but there were times when I doubted if that were true. Writing this book is one of those things that I didn't think I could do. I felt like it would be too hard compiling my Mom's words of wisdom, writing them all down to make a book, then printing the book, marketing it—it was an overwhelming process, to say the least. But I kept hearing my Mom's voice saying, "You can do anything you put your mind to." "Keep at it," she would say, "and you'll get it done." My Mom instilled in me a sense of pride about myself by always affirming me as a person, correcting me when I went astray, and being a good example of how far having a positive outlook on life can take you. I remember looking in the mirror one morning while getting ready for church and picking out my afro and then patting it, trying to make it look even, when my Mom came up and said, "You look beautiful." I said, "Yeah, you're just saying that because you're ready to leave for church." Her response was, "I wouldn't say it if I didn't mean it." She stood there watching me in the mirror for another minute or so, and then she said, "Now we really do have to leave." By then, I was ready to go whether my afro was perfect or not because my Mom had affirmed me. I have a ritual now where I look in the mirror and tell myself that I am successful, beautiful, and worthy. Whenever I would let my Mom know of a challenge facing me, she would respond, "What's the problem? I think you can do that." I would analyze her actual question, What is the problem?, and then figure out a solution. My Mom stopped actually telling me what to do a long time ago. She would encourage me to figure it out for myself.

Even during the time that I spent with my Mom during her final days, there was little left for her to pass on to me because she had already done so. She had taught me about maintaining a home, finances, love and respect for God, yourself, and others, accountability, and countless other life lessons; so what I was able to get from those last few weeks was the ability to recognize the gift she had placed in me and to dig deep within my soul and apply those lessons in order to live the courageous life I was meant to.

Lesson 7: Not Going to Church Isn't an Option If You're Going to Live in My House

Let the Church Say Amen

Growing up in my Mom's household, my brother and I learned early on that not going to church wasn't an option. We went to church at least twice a week, once for the midweek service and then again on Sunday morning. Depending on what was going on, we might have another service to attend on Sunday afternoon--for example, the church or pastor's anniversary—or whenever there was a fifth Sunday we would attend the Sunday School Union. The Sunday School Union was when a group of the local churches within the same district got together at rotating churches to worship and have fellowship. On those occasions, I often had a poem to recite or a song to sing. It was at church that I learned some valuable Christian lessons about how to treat others and how to serve God and His people. I attended a small country church where everybody knew one another. It was often filled with family and friends, and occasionally we would have some out-of-town guests or visitors from neighboring churches. This was an environment where we sang the old gospel hymns, the mothers of the church mentored us, stained-glass windows looked back at the congregation, and the minister preached a soul-stirring message that was just what we needed to take us through the week to come. The church at that time served a valuable purpose within the community. It created a safe place for people to assemble and not only find spiritual nourishment for their soul but physical sustenance as well. We felt a real sense of community back then. My experience growing up in church has helped me become a more tolerant person and embrace the concept of loving my neighbor as myself.

    I am grateful to my Mom for taking me to church; and because of her example, I now take my son to church. I would watch my Mom usher on Sundays, prepare food, and then serve local and out-of-town guests who were attending our church for a special service. Like my Mom, I, too, became an usher in two of the churches that I have attended as an adult. I am grateful for my Mom's influence on my journey in knowing and understanding God. I believe it was my Mom's faith that got her through the difficult time during her illness. It was her relationship with God that allowed her to be at peace with those things that she could not change and to trust that everything would work out the way it was supposed to. I, too, have the same peace that I'm on the right spiritual path and that things are working out in my favor. Because of her example, I have taken the love that I have acquired for God and expanded my knowledge of and relationship with Him. My prayer for you is that you be strengthened by your faith, encouraged by the love of those closest to you, and surrounded by the peace of God that surpasses all understanding. Amen.

Lesson 8: Behold the Beauty in All Things

The Human Spirit

My Mom saw the beauty and worth in all things, and she enjoyed having nice belongings. She not only saw the beauty in things, but she saw the beauty and worth in people. Everyone was important to my Mom, from babies to the very oldest. She would always acknowledge you and make you feel special. She would acknowledge your accomplishments with a card that oftentimes accompanied money for birthdays, holidays, or graduation. She would honor your presence by singling you out from the crowd and by saying something nice to or about you or someone close to you, like, "How is your mother?" or "How are those babies today?" Recently, my cousin Adrian posted on Facebook a picture of his Dad in memory of his death, and I responded by saying how much I missed his Dad (my great uncle); he replied, "I miss your Mom. She was always so nice to me." That is a very common response from folks about my Mom.

My Mom enjoyed the outdoors. She would work out in her yard for hours at a time planting flowers, weeding, and doing other landscape projects with the intent to make it beautiful for her enjoyment and for the passersby. It seems I have acquired from my Mom that same taste for the finer things in life. I love nice clothes, furniture, and cars. One thing that I learned over time from my Mom is that you can have beautiful things without having to take out a second mortgage on your home to get them. My Mom was really into bargain shopping. She would buy everything on sale. She would shop in the fancy department stores; in fact, Belk was one of her favorite stores, but the item would have to be on sale or at least be reasonably priced for her to buy it. She could find beautiful treasures at second-hand stores. People would comment on how beautifully decorated my Mom's home was, and little did they know that the majority of the furnishings cost a fraction of what they were worth because of how skillful she was at bargain shopping. I had a high school teacher who would say to me all the time, "Beauty is as beauty does." I believe my Mom was a beautiful person inside and out, and so she surrounded herself and others with beauty.

    In her final days and weeks, she exhibited that same beauty and grace. Not only did she want to look her best on the outside, by getting her hair done so that she could wear those nice turban hats that matched her gown, but I experienced the beauty of her selflessness when she still put others before herself. Early on, she wanted to make sure that

I purchased plenty of thank-you and acknowledgment cards, so that I could respond to everyone who expressed concern about her during her illness. She also gave me the most precious gift of beauty by allowing me to be a part of her last days here on earth. During the process, she was still imparting wisdom with her instruction on how to prepare special meals, how to care for her as a patient, and how to manage finances, as I would write her bills. But, most importantly, I learned how to put myself and my needs aside just for a season, in order to experience a very real human experience, the transition from life to death. I will never forget those moments as they will forever play out in my mind and as I behold my Mom, in all her beauty, in her final days here on earth.

Lesson 9: The Power of Giving

My Mom was the first person to teach me the concept of giving. She would never let me take money from people in return for doing something nice for them. Her belief was that you help people because it's the right thing to do, not because there's something in it for you. She wanted me to get into the habit of being kind with no strings attached so it would become second nature because she recognized that the reward from that individual could never measure up to the greater benefits you would receive from God for helping out your fellow human being in need. Some of the many benefits of giving unconditionally that I've discovered include the mere satisfaction of knowing that you've helped someone and that good things are given back to you in return. I have lived at least the last fifteen years of my life in the giving mode. I have found the Bible to be very true on this account: when you give of your time, talent, and treasure, you will be tremendously blessed, just as I have been. Giving also opens up your hand and your heart to be able to receive. It exposes you to a world of possibilities. Don't limit your opportunities by trying to hold on to your resources. Whatever God has blessed you with is for you to share with others.

You may be thinking, now I know that God blesses us as individuals and intends for us to keep those things for ourselves. Yes, He does bless us, but even with the individual blessing, there is still room to share. I watched my Mom perform little acts of kindness, like giving her freshly cut vegetables away to those in need, which would send her back to the family garden to glean more in order to prepare for our Sunday dinner. Giving is the gift that keeps on giving. When you give something away, you get so much in return and oftentimes not in the way that you expect it. Practice the art of giving yourself away in order to be used. When you give yourself away, you are saying that it's not about you, but something much bigger than yourself.

My Mom taught me that giving is a condition of the heart. You have to want to see people doing well. She would say that there's always a need, and your job is to find out what it is and go about meeting that need. Do as much as you can and leave the rest for someone else to come along and do. For example, my Mom would say, "If someone needs an entire set of clothes, and all you can provide is shoes, then by all means, give shoes. But don't walk away because you feel the need is too great for you to accomplish on your own." One of the benefits of giving that I've noticed is a deeper emotional connectedness to yourself and to others. When I give to others first, I pass on feelings of love and compassion. As a result, I feel better about myself and others; and before I know it, I'm creating positive energy. Another benefit of giving is that life becomes bigger than you. When your life becomes about serving others, you'll find that life is much more fulfilling and purposeful.

My Mom modeled this lesson yet again in her final days. She was much less focused on her own healing and more concerned that I was equipped to handle life once she was gone. I learned firsthand how to unselfishly put myself aside to help others; and when you do, your life is all the richer.

Lesson 10: Gratitude Is an Attitude, and Practice Makes Perfect

Expressing Gratitude

Expressing gratitude is one way of remaining humble. I can remember many stories of gratitude that my Mom shared with me. However, there is one that stands out. Once after receiving a not-so-great Christmas present from a relative, I was going on and on about how terrible the gift was, and how it was useless, and what was this person thinking by passing on such a crappy gift. My Mom calmly sat me down and explained to me that I needed to be grateful for the gift and the person giving the gift. She went on to say that acknowledging the person who gave you the gift is just as important, if not more so, because you are recognizing the good in that person, their thoughtfulness, kindness, and generosity; and when you acknowledge those characteristics in others, you honor the same characteristics in yourself. After that talk, I never looked solely at the gift anymore, but more deeply into the person and the meaning of gift giving. Today I am grateful for every gift big and small, and I am especially grateful for the person who gave me the gift. This is a lesson that I have passed down to my dear son, Caleb.

What are you grateful for? Studies show that when we express gratitude, it makes us feel good about ourselves, those around us, and the world and causes us to give more. My Mom would take me with her on her routine visits to see the sick and shut in. We would take food to them, and we did the household chores that they were not able to do because of their frailties. The people whom my Mom would help along the way would show their gratitude with cards, letters, gifts during the holidays, and they would always verbally express their appreciation for Mom's kind deeds. I believe that in some way my Mom felt that part of her purpose in life was to help make life better for people, and she went about it one small deed at a time because she was grateful for her own blessings and wanted to pass that on. I practice my attitude of gratitude daily by saying out loud those things that I am grateful for.

My Mom loved her two grandsons and her nieces and nephews and lived out her gratitude for them in deed. For a few summers she would host seven or eight kids for a week or so to give their parents a break. The kids loved the experience of being able to run free out in the country, playing with their cousins and eating everything in sight. I watched my Mom perform these acts of love and kindness for those she loved, and it taught me among other things the importance of demonstrating your gratitude toward others as well as expressing kind words.

My Mom was grateful for so many things. Her family was at the top of the list. She was thankful for the time that she got to spend with her many friends and relatives; even at the end when she was too sick to respond, she appreciated their presence. She never turned company away; it lifted her spirit in many ways to be surrounded by so much love. Because of the impact my Mom's life had on me, I, too, am grateful for the small blessings, as well as the big ones, as they all come together to shape my perspective on what it means to really have a grateful spirit.

Just as my Mom showed me, God wants us to be grateful for the big and little things; then He will bless us with bigger things. Make a list of five things that you are grateful for, and experience your heart meter register off the chart.

I will share with you five things that I am grateful for:

1. I am grateful to my Mom for living her life as a positive example to me and those around her, so that I may know and experience how to love and serve those around me, and so that others' lives may be enriched by the process.

2. I am grateful to you for taking the time to read my book. I pray that you will discover the real meaning for your life after the death of a loved one.

3. I am grateful for my son Caleb as he continues to grow spiritually. He is a child of great wisdom and depth. His compassion toward others makes my heart glad.

4. I am grateful for the opportunity to have been given the wisdom and the tools I need to live a meaningful life.

5. I am grateful for everyone who has crossed my path throughout the years, for you have inspired me in some way to keep moving forward on this journey, as tiresome as it may get at times. The goal is to keep moving forward in love and service.

About the Author

Angie Steele is a freelance writer and an advocate for positive children's programming. She has a passion for television programming and has managed the live production of a major television ministry here in the Raleigh/Durham area with programming aired nationally. She has written stage plays and is the producer of a children's animation series called the Adventures of Warner D.

Angiemsteeleinc.com
Durham, NC 27712

To order copies of this publication, visit us at

www.angiemsteele.com

or email

info@angiemsteele.com

www.ingramcontent.com/pod-product-compliance
Lightning Source LLC
Chambersburg PA
CBHW061302040426
42444CB00010B/2478